NATIONAL
GEOGRAPHI

What's on the Road?

Norman Yu

What's on the road?

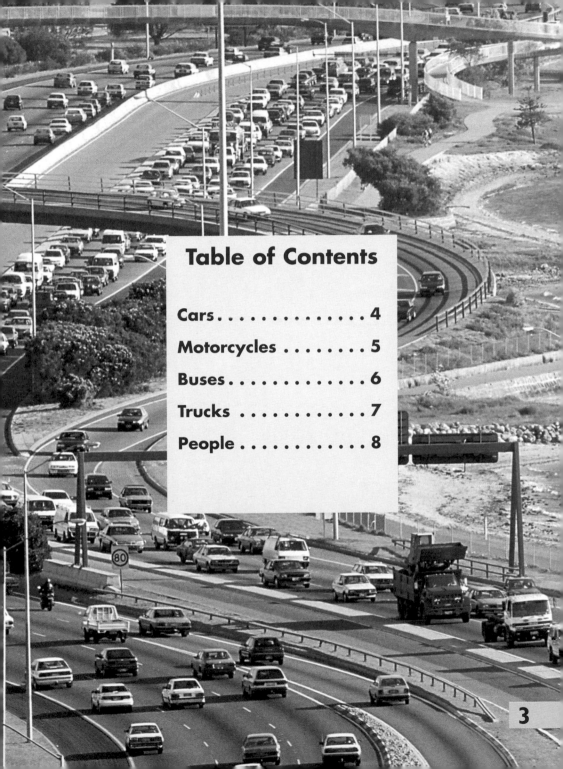

Table of Contents

There are **cars** on the road.

There are **motorcycles** on the road.

There are **buses** on the road.

There are **trucks** on the road.

There are **people** on the road.